ZANY, BRAINY ANIMALS

HOW ANIMALS ADAPT

DR. ASHLEY WARD AND ANDY ROWLAND

PowerKiDS press

Published in 2026
by The Rosen Publishing Group, Inc.
2544 Clinton Street, Buffalo, NY 14224

First published in Great Britain in 2024 by Wayland

Editors: Elise Short, Jenni Lazell
Designer: Rachel Lawston

Cataloging-in-Publication Data

Names: Ward, Ashley, author. | Rowland, Andy, 1962-, illustrator.
Title: How animals adapt / by Dr. Ashley Ward, illustrated by Andy Rowland.
Description: Buffalo, NY : PowerKids Press, 2026. | Series: Zany, brainy animals | Includes glossary and index.
Identifiers: ISBN 9781499454093 (pbk.) | ISBN 9781499454109 (library bound) | ISBN 9781499454116 (ebook)
Subjects: LCSH: Animals--Adaptation--Juvenile literature. | Adaptation (Biology)--Juvenile literature.
Classification: LCC QH546.W373 2026 | DDC 591.4--dc23

Manufactured in the United States of America

CPSIA Compliance Information: Batch #CSPK26. For further information contact Rosen Publishing at 1-800-237-9932.

Picture credits:
Alamy: Biosphoto 22; Keren Su/China Span: David Tipling Photo Library 28.
Shutterstock: Mark Bridger 20tr; Luca Cavallari 23; Jeff Caverly 20bl; Steve Collender 26; Andy Deitsch 27t; Iliuta Goean 24bl; Hayder55 19; Thanakorn Hongphan 13bl; Stewart Innes 5c; Eric Isselee back cover, 11t, 15b, 21tr, 25bl; Jukka Jantunen 7b; Zapylaiev Kostiantyn 12bl; Kubais 14; Don Landwehrie 6t; Ondrej Prosicky 4; Stormarm 27b; SubAtomicScope 9b; Ali A Suliman 18; Travel Media Productions front cover; Vojce 25tr; Peter Wey 16.

CONTENTS

HOW DO ANIMALS ADAPT?

Life can be a challenge for animals and one of the most important things they have to deal with is **CHANGE**. This change might happen quickly, such as the appearance of a predator or a sudden switch in the weather, or it could happen more slowly, as happens when each season gives way to the next or animals pass down survival traits to their babies. But the most important thing in all these cases is that animals can **ADAPT**.

Being good at adapting is the secret of success for animals. In this book, we're going to explore some **INCREDIBLE** examples of just how animals adapt and how this helps them to not just SURVIVE but to THRIVE!

TALES FROM THE LAB

Understanding animal behavior is not an easy task. First, scientists watch animals living their life. That's how they get their ideas. Then they test these ideas by running experiments. If they're lucky, they'll find out something that no one has ever known about animals, which is the most exciting result possible! In this book, you'll find many amazing discoveries about how animals adapt.

SLEEPING IN SNOW

For animals like the polar bear that live in the far north of the Arctic Circle, winter is **NO JOKE**. Temperatures can drop to almost -58°F (-50°C) compared to the average temp of 21.2°F (-6°C). The animals that the bears eat, such as seals, leave when the temperature falls. Polar bears can cope with cold weather, but this is hard–even for them!

To survive in these tough conditions, the bears do something very smart. They dig down into deep snowdrifts, make themselves a den and ... **TAKE IT SLOW!** They slow down and don't move around as much in order to preserve their energy until summertime. This special kind of state is known as **HIBERNATION**.

Hibernating animals don't need to eat. Their bodies keep going by using up fat stores. Some hibernating animals, such as the Arctic ground squirrel, slow down so much that their heart beats more slowly, and their breathing rate drops too. To save energy, the Arctic ground squirrel even decreases its body temperature to a chilly 26.6°F (-3°C)!

TALES FROM THE LAB

To find out about Arctic ground squirrels' behaviors during hibernation, in 2001, a team of researchers from the University of Alaska Fairbanks placed tiny radio transmitters on 14 adult squirrels that could track the squirrels' temperature under their skin, before releasing them back into the wild. From this, the researchers learned how a squirrel's body changes during hibernation, and how it uses its energy to survive the cold winter months.

FOOD-FUELED FIENDISHNESS

You might have seen grasshoppers bouncing around in fields at some time or other, and if so, you'd probably agree that they don't seem particularly troublesome. But there's one particular kind of grasshopper, known as a locust, that can cause serious damage.

Most of the time, locusts don't do any harm at all. They keep to themselves, munching leaves and living a quiet life. The problems start when the food supplies start to dry up and the locusts are forced together in shrinking patches of food.

When they cluster and jostle together, a strange change happens, and the locusts transform from peaceful loners into a marching army of ravenous eating machines. They are better able to find food together by covering more ground. It also helps protect them from predators.

If any locust in the swarm decides it needs a rest and stops marching, the others show no sympathy. In fact, the ones behind will **CHEW ITS BUM OFF!**

When locusts gather like this, there might be billions of starving insects marching relentlessly over huge areas of land, eating everything that's green and reducing farmers' crops to ruin.

TALES FROM THE LAB

Locusts are a huge problem for lots of people around the world, so working out why they have learned to adapt and flip into their swarming mode is vitally important. Researchers at the University of Sydney in Australia made an amazing discovery about this by tickling locusts with a paintbrush. They found that if you stroke their legs, replicating what happens when locusts are forced together, they transform into aggressive, swarming locusts.

STAYING OUT OF HARM'S WAY

It's a fact of life that some animals face a harder start in life than others. Take tadpoles, for instance. Some of these little wigglers grow up in ponds where there's not much for them to worry about. Others spend their early days in pools living alongside predators, such as aquatic salamanders, that would very much like to eat them.

But these threatened tadpoles have a trick up their sleeve! To foil the nasty salamanders, they grow in a completely different way to their cousins in the safer ponds. They grow **EXTRA-LARGE, GIANT HEADS** that the salamanders find it hard to grab on to and swallow.

Just to make doubly sure, the tadpoles behave differently too. Rather than actively flitting around like regular tadpoles, they **KEEP STILL** for much of the time. This is because being busy can attract the attention of their salamander predators, but it might also be that it's harder to swim when you've got a giant head!

TALES FROM THE LAB

Scientists interested in the adaptability of these little tadpoles wanted to know what happens when you take them from their predator-infested environment and put them in a safe place, far away from the salamanders. Sure enough, they quickly started behaving like regular tadpoles, and even their giant heads started to shrink!

SINGING IN THE CITY

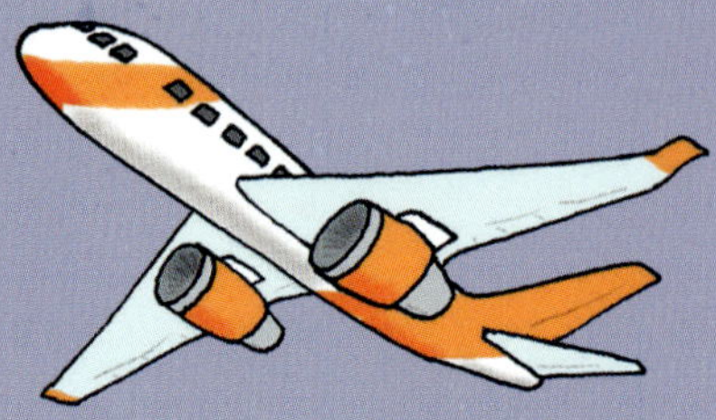

Sadly, some of the changes that animals experience are caused by us. But animals still need to adapt to survive–and one of the best examples of this is how some birds, such as sparrows, adapt to living in cities.

Imagine you're a sparrow and you've made your home in a big , noisy city like London, UK; Mumbai, India; or Beijing, China. You know that you need to sing to protect your home and you also need to sing to attract a mate. However, the sounds of traffic and trains and alarms and all the other noises found in a city threaten to drown out your little voice. So what do you do? You change your song!

Ornithologists (people who study birds) have found that because the sound of traffic is at a low frequency (deep, bass sounds), the birds counteract this by singing higher-pitched songs to get their message across. Not only this, but some city birds have begun to sing at night when there's less traffic!

TALES FROM THE LAB

In 2020, during the COVID-19 pandemic, scientists in Germany took advantage of an airport closing down to study the effects of noise on birds. Before the airport closed, studies showed some birds singing earlier in the morning to avoid the noise. The scientists recorded birds in various locations and analyzed the recordings to see which birds they heard and when. They found that some birds started singing later when the noise was gone.

GOING UNDERGROUND

How would you feel about living underground? Probably not that great, but some animals have found that there's a great life to enjoy by burrowing.

It's safe underground and there's plenty of food, if you know where to look. But it can be difficult to live a life that involves almost constant digging, where there's less air to breathe and no light. Consider the mole, an animal that has not only adapted to this way of life but has become the **MASTER OF UNDERGROUND LIVING!**

These **LITTLE DIGGERS** are amazing, with their powerful forelimbs and shovel-shaped hands, they can dig 3 feet (1 m) of tunnel through hard-packed soil in just 10 minutes! Since there's no light in their burrows, they've gradually lost their eyesight, relying instead on other incredibly sharp senses, particularly smell and touch, to find their worm prey in the darkness. Moles even have toxic chemicals in their saliva that they use to **STUN** worms and stop them from wiggling off into the darkness!

Researchers are interested in the many amazing adaptations shown by mammals that live underground, such as the chemicals in their blood that allow them to breathe when there's hardly any fresh air. The naked mole rat, a distant cousin of the mole, has lost the ability to feel pain and doesn't suffer from serious diseases, such as cancer.

BLENDING IN

Unlike some of the more showy people you might know, most animals try not to draw attention to themselves. Such creatures might have any number of different reasons to dodge the limelight, but these usually boil down to either remaining unnoticed by scary predators or being better able to sneak up on their own prey.

Some animals can change the color of their whole body to match their environment, a nifty trick known as camouflage. The peacock flounder, a funny kind of flatfish that lives in warm ocean regions, is one of the most impressive. Whenever the peacock flounder moves to a different patch, it changes color in less than 10 seconds!

Even more impressively, even when sneaky scientists decided to test the peacock flounder by putting the fish on a black and white checkerboard, the fish became black and white!

TALES FROM THE LAB

The natural world is a great source of inspiration for scientists. By learning how the peacock flounder's skin manages to change color so rapidly, engineers hope to design artificial materials that could be used to coat buildings so that they change color at different times of day: brilliant white to reflect the sun's heat at the hottest time of day, or dark to absorb sunshine at colder times.

DESERT DEFENSES

Deserts, such as the Sahara in North Africa, are one of the most challenging places for animals to live. There's very little water or food, and there's not even much shade in a place where temperatures regularly reach more than 104°F (40°C). You might imagine that no animal could cope with this, but consider this one: the camel!

Camels are beautifully adapted for life in this most hostile of environments. They have thick fur on their backs to keep the sun off, and very thin fur on their bellies and legs to allow heat to escape and keep them cool.

And what about food and drink? Camels store fat in the humps on their backs, which they use as a food reserve for times when there's not much to eat. It's a bit like taking a packed lunch around with them. And while they might not get the chance to drink often, when they do, they make the most of it, slurping down a third of their body weight in water!

TALES FROM THE LAB

Animals give off water all the time when they sweat and when they breathe. That's why when you breathe on a mirror it mists up. This is from water vapor in your breath. Biologists interested in how camels conserve their precious water have found that camels almost never sweat, and they can close their nostrils and recycle the water vapor that collects there!

ANIMAL DOCTORS

If you were a bird, what do you think you'd make your nest out of? Maybe some sticks, a bit of grass, or maybe some comfy moss? In Mexico City, house finches turn their beaks up at these kinds of things and instead build their nests out of cigarette butts. **YUCK!**

Why do they do this? We know that smoking kills and so, apparently, do birds. The cigarette butts may be stinky but they're also full of a poisonous chemical called nicotine. This kills the **NASTY, BLOODSUCKING LICE** that usually live in their nests and that can harm their chicks.

This is an example of animals finding their own medicines, and there's even a word for it, although the word is long: zoopharmacognosy.

Examples of this include the apes, monkeys, and even birds that seek out and eat nasty-tasting medicinal leaves or toxic beetles to kill bugs that live in their insides. And bears are among a host of animals who rub their fur with particular kinds of leaves to keep biting insects away.

People have copied animals by watching the medicines that they use for thousands of years. In Kenya, women, as well as female elephants, seek out the leaves of a particular tree, which is thought to help them during childbirth.

GOING HUNGRY

Caves can be found in many parts of the world, hidden deep underground. It's tough to stay alive in these dark, cold places but even so, there are animals that have managed it.

Take the olm, for instance. This creature is a kind of salamander that has adapted to cave life and can be found underground throughout Central Europe.

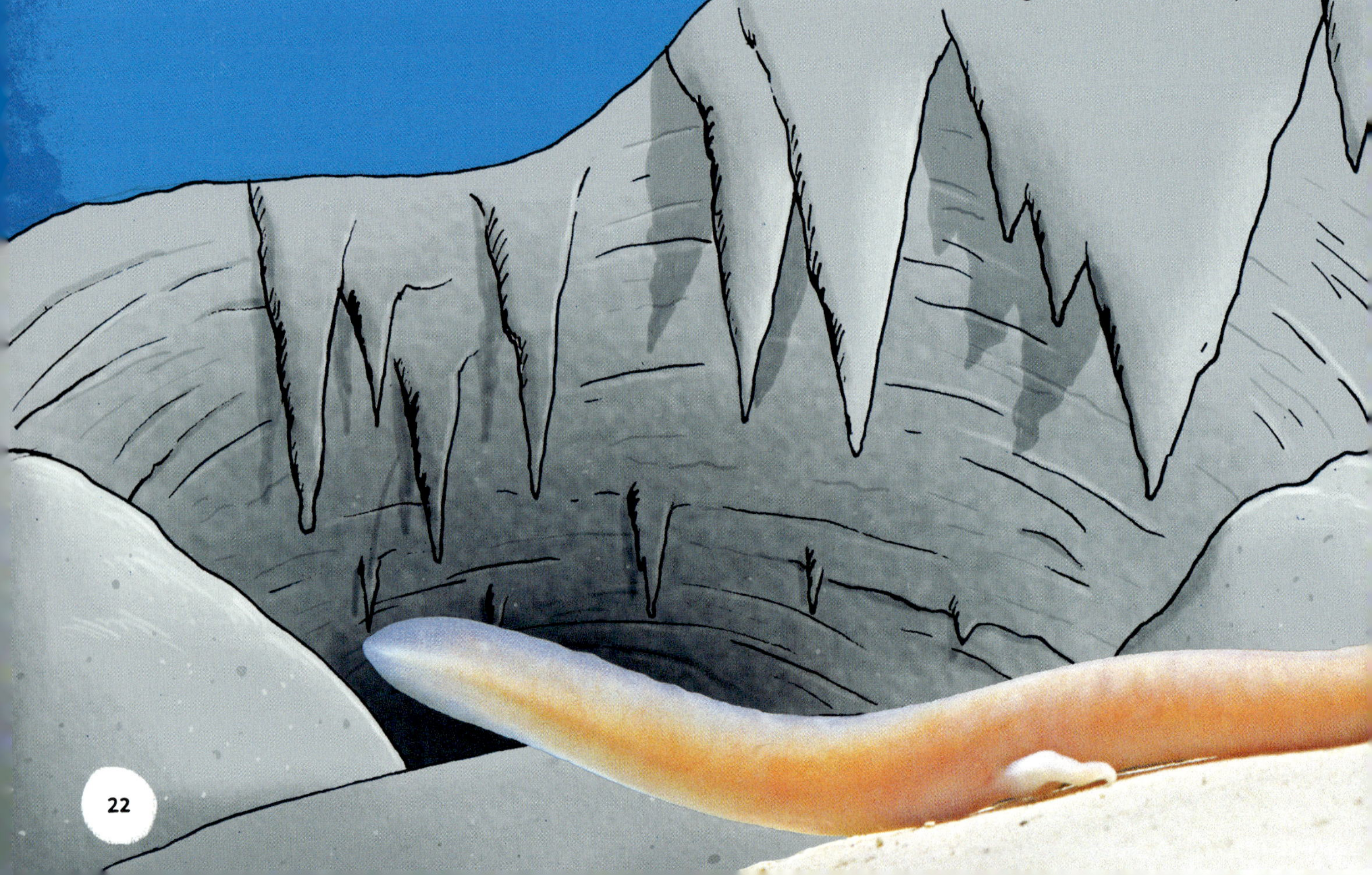

Like many other cave-dwelling animals that live in permanent darkness, the olm's eyes no longer work. It relies on its other senses for finding its way. It has also lost the colors that many salamanders have, and instead, it's plain pink in color. Its color and appearance, along with its little arms and legs, have led to it to be nicknamed the "human fish."

How long would you be able to go without eating? A human can survive one to two months as long as they have water. How long do you think an olm can go without eating? The answer, incredibly, is **10 YEARS!** They achieve this by living life very, very slowly and as a result, these little amphibians can live for more than **100 years!**

DECIDING WHO TO BE

Coral gobies are tiny but very colorful fish that live on tropical reefs around the world. Their small size means that there are lots of other fish out there that might eat them. To stay safe they almost never venture far from the coral they live in, hiding among the cracks and crevices.

There is a time when a coral goby must leave the safety of its hideaway, and that's when it wants to find a mate. Going any distance from home puts the coral goby at **TERRIBLE** risk, so to help make sure that the journey isn't too long, they've come up with one of the **MOST AMAZING ADAPTATIONS** in the animal kingdom!

When they find another coral goby who looks like it might be a good mate, they change sex to compliment the other. So if they meet a female, they become male, or if they meet a male, they become female! The bigger goby of the two, usually a male, will become female when a female mate is not present. By doing this, they make sure they don't have to wander as far to find a suitable mate.

There are quite a few fish that change sex as they grow, though few are as adaptable as the coral goby. Some, like cleaner wrasse, start as females and transform into males while others, such as clownfish, start off as males and later become females. Biologists are interested in this because it shows how animal bodies stay changeable enough to adapt.

MARINE IGUANAS

A special group of islands off the coast of South America is known as the Galápagos. One of the things that makes these islands so special is the amazing animals that live there, many of which aren't found anywhere else.

The marine iguana is one of the most incredible creatures of the Galápagos. Their iguana ancestors lived across the water on the South American mainland, where they lived in tropical forests and ate fruit. It's thought that some of these got washed out to sea on fallen trees and ended up in the Galápagos like shipwrecked sailors.

The new arrivals faced all sorts of problems, not least of which was that their favorite fruity food can't be found on the Galápagos. There is plenty of one food around these islands though—seaweed. To get at this, the iguanas had to adapt.

Rather than sitting in the branches of tropical trees, the iguanas became expert swimmers, diving down to get at the tasty seaweed on the seabed. The water is cold, however, so marine iguanas have to leave the water to bask in the sun and warm up. And if you were to ever see them basking, you'd notice that they sneeze quite often. They don't have colds. They do this to expel the salt they pick up from their ocean diet!

PENGUIN PARADES

Antarctica is the coldest place on Earth. And if that wasn't enough, fierce winds scour the land and snowstorms swirl. It's not the easiest place to live, and yet some animals still make Antarctica their home.

Penguins are incredibly well adapted to life in this freezing environment. To hold on to their body heat, they have a thick layer of feathers that lock together and special networks of blood vessels that prevent them from losing too much warmth through their feet. In the breeding season, they hold their delicate eggs on top of their feet to stop them getting chilled on the frozen ground.

Even so, when it gets really cold, penguins gather in huddles, pressed close together to keep each other warm. Amazingly, this is so effective that the penguins in the middle of the huddle can overheat if they're not careful!

To avoid this, the penguins switch places, so that the hot birds from the middle of the huddle go to the outside to cool down, while the colder ones at the edge of the huddle head inward to warm up! Penguins keep moving to make sure they stay at the perfect temperature.

GLOSSARY

Adaptation the way a species changes over time to become better suited to its environment

Amphibian a cold-blooded animal with a skeleton inside its body. Amphibians can live both on land and in water.

Behavior the way in which a person or animal acts

Blend in to look or seem the same as the surroundings and not be easily noticeable

Breed to make babies

Burrow to dig; also a hole in the ground dug by an animal to live in

Camouflage the way that the color or shape of an animal or plant appears to blend with its surroundings in order to prevent it from being seen and attacked

Hibernation a type of deep sleep some animals enter into in winter. Their heart rate and breathing slows, and their temperature drops

Mammal a warm-blooded animal with fur or hair on its skin and a skeleton inside its body. Mammal mothers produce milk to feed their babies.

Mate one of a pair of animals that have babies together

Poisonous a harmful or deadly substance

Predator an animal that hunts other animals for food

Prey an animal that is hunted for food, usually by another animal

Swarm a huge group of insects moving together in the same direction

Zoopharmacognosy the way animals find and use their own medicines

FURTHER INFORMATION

Books

Funny Bums, Freaky Beaks: and Other Incredible Creature Features
by Alex Morss and Sean Taylor (Welbeck, 2022)

Hiding Away
by Anne O'Daly (Brown Bear, 2025)

Stinky Skunks and Other Animal Adaptations (Disgusting and Dreadful Science)
by Barbara Taylor (Wayland, 2021)

Websites

Explore zoology, the study of animals, through articles and games:
www.amnh.org/explore/ology/zoology

Watch a video that explains adaptations here:
https://naturalhistory.si.edu/education/teaching-resources/life-science/explore-animal-adaptations

INDEX